THE CASE FOR
Honesty

Anca Tudorascu

The Author asserts the moral right to be identified
as the author of this work

ISBN-13: 978-2919946709

Copyright © Anca Tudorascu, 2017

Illustrations copyright © Anca Tudorascu, 2017

All rights reserved, including the right of
reproduction in whole or in part in any form

In loving memory of my maternal grandparents

your life is your life
don't let it be clubbed into dank submission.
be on the watch.
there are ways out.
there is a light somewhere.

    (The Laughing Heart by Charles Bukowski)

Contents

Introduction 1

A simpler way of living 3

This side of consciousness 10

View towards the ocean 13

Happy journey 16

Fall into the inner darkness 18

Animals are nourishment 21

Childhood and other musings 26

Promise you will never leave me behind 35

Anatomy of a job announcement 37

Who can break this cycle? 42

Equality 48

Painting, living and other lost arts 50

Our turn, tomorrow? 53

Imprisoned souls 57

An exercise in positive thinking 60

View from the meadow 63

New spring 67

Bread and circuses 69

Be the best that you can be 74

Whatever happened to critical thinking 80

Introduction

Through the following pages, I have set out to explore, with as much honesty as I could muster, issues that are hidden, forgotten, or ignored in my own life or the life of those around me, from family members to society at large. By no means exhaustive, this personal account of ideas and experiences deals with topics such as simple living, money management, family dynamics, animals, depression, to name just a few.

I hope the ideas presented here will stay with you longer than the time taken to read them, and they will encourage you to examine with similar honesty your own life views and experiences. While, as far as I am aware, introspection has not killed anyone, a grain of it would surely prevent many instances of cruelty in our dealings with one another.

It may happen that you will disagree with some of the views developed in the book. That is fine for two reasons: firstly, no person is a holder of the absolute truth; secondly, when two or more persons agree on everything with one another, it means that someone is not exercising the intrinsically human ability of thinking.

The texts that follow should be understood as the beginning of a deeper conversation.

A simpler way of living

I was lucky to spend most of my early childhood with my grandparents on a homestead tucked away under the Carpathians, in the Romanian countryside. The more I travel through life, the more I become aware of the great impact our experiences during the early years of our life have on the rest of our existence. Sometimes I believe that all I have been doing so far has been trying to re-enact those early childhood days, which are forever lost except that they linger in my thoughts and in my profound being.

One of the things my grandparents and life on their homestead have taught me is that we do not need much to live and to be happy. Nowadays most people live in urban areas, crammed in small apartments, hold full-time jobs in order to get money, which in turn allows them to provide for their needs and those of their children. They are disconnected from nature as a source of food and life. They do not have any skills that would allow them to live from the land, and the great majority of them do not own any land either. Total alienation from the most basic source of life. Which means that they need to go to school for increasingly longer periods of time, hold jobs for a life-time and get into debt in order to amass the necessary money to purchase all that they need or want from large commercial entities whose only raison d'être is profit. Lots of it.

This scenario does not make for a safe life or for a particularly joyous existence. This is because most of us are dependent on a large intricate system, upon which we have no control, for our most basic necessities. It would be enough for our society to be hit by serious economic crisis, by war, or by some natural disaster, and many of us would be reduced to begging in the streets, would lose our shelter and the only source of our livelihood, our *sacred* jobs.

But how many people are pondering the perils of their situation? Not too many, I presume, if it is to judge by the happy ways in which they part with their hard-earned money on many frivolities, by the fact that they consider normal to dig themselves deep into debt for a car or for much more home that they need or really afford, not to mention even more outrageous reasons for which people get into debt, such as trips or consumer goods.

To come back to my grandparents' homestead, I consider myself lucky to have experienced a very simple lifestyle early on, poor by today's standards, but for me at the time, endlessly rich and happy. As a result, now I know that owning a piece of land and mastering the necessary skills to cultivate the land for food, to raise and butcher animals is much more sustainable wealth than most people have access to today.

Land ownership has always been considered real wealth and the rich people have always owned most of it. The situation has not changed to this day, except that you do not hear about it too often. The ordinary person is blinded by shiny and useless consumer goods, the latest gadgets and pretty things, while the well to do and powerful of this world still invest in land and real estate, except that they can afford it, right? I invite you to get out of town for a drive in the surrounding countryside. Do you ever wonder who owns those lush and vast terrains, while you and I live crammed in a few square meters? I believe not many people own those lands. It is probably safe to say that a tiny percentage of privileged families hold the property title to the majority of the land of *your* country. And so you see, *your* country is a nice figure of speech that does not reflect at all most people's reality.

I will not get into all the obstacles our social construct is placing, on purpose, in front of the people who would want to have access to a piece of life-sustaining land, even if they were not lucky enough to be born in a wealthy family. I would just tell you, don't let the difficulty of the endeavour deter you from persevering. Before all things, it is important to distinguish between what has real value in this world, and what has not. Health, family, (real!) education and skills, a shelter, and if possible a piece of land - these should be most valued by you.

If you know what has value you will not waste your time chasing the fake bounties because, as you may have discovered or you are about to discover as you reach middle age, human life is a finite time and space that we have at our disposal to express our unique light. All the difficulty lies within this constraint. Time is also a big equalizer. We all have limited time at our disposal and remaining aware of the finish line may help us focus more intensely on the experience of living. Maybe this is one of truths the big religions of the world want to communicate to us. Some have used their time to create masterpieces, others to make scientific breakthroughs, yet others to raise a family or to care for their fellow humans through their hardship. All of these endeavours are praiseworthy. What path have you chosen?

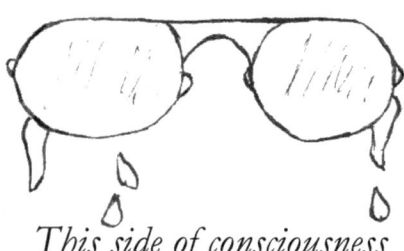

This side of consciousness

How could I look with optimism towards the future, when deep in the dark corners of my life and of my mind, he would be lying on cold cement in desperation or hiding from all that he had known; when he is degraded, frightened, defenceless and lonely? How can I hope to build a life, like I was doing, when another younger life is tortured and threatened with extinction?

Drama is occurring every second in this harsh world we live in, but until it touches us in our very flesh we forget that it exists. We see it on TV, we read about it in the media, we even passingly see it on the corner of a street, but it all seems unreal, like a made-up thing, until it hits us in the face.

Then, we go right into denial mode. Surely this could not happen to me or to my family. Since drama isn't real, it cannot affect us. We don't know what other people have done so that scary things happen to them, but surely none of that could ever occur in our own lives. No. No.

But well it does. Of course, one day sooner or later, drama is bound to visit us as well. Provided that we breathe long enough on this solitary and god-forsaken rock, the Evil will touch us all someday. Some ordinary day, without any apparent warning, though warning is always sent galore to those who stay awake and listen, listen attentively to the background whispers of life.

One ordinary day, we go about our business in the usual fashion, not too happy, not too sad, mumbling some complaints about frivolous matters. And, then, just like that, a bright light is switched on, and the blood is exposed for all to see on the living room wall. It is a wound that grows and grows, and it doesn't want to stop or fade away. It's bright and ugly, surreal and obscene. What is this doing in our life?

This *is* life. Earlier you were dreaming. Now you have woken up and realized that the nightmare is on this side of consciousness. Welcome to your reality! Too tough to swallow? Too indecent for your exquisite little taste? Life has all those "qualities", but we don't want to see them, because it is much less painful to go about it in an ignorant, naive, hopeful manner, armed with our rosy-glasses and a glass of wine, like a drunken comedian passing through a war zone. *Watch out not to step on a grenade on your way home, you poor bastard! Cheers!*

View towards the ocean

Looking out of the window, I can see water as far as the horizon. I hear unfamiliar birds in the nearby trees and fill my lungs with fresh air. A rooster greets the day in the distance. The red roofs of the houses interrupt here and there the monotony of the rich vegetation that clings to even the most abrupt sides of the mountain.

Am I in paradise or on a piece of land lost in the middle of the ocean?

This is the Island of Madeira, closer to Africa than to my home, the European mainland. The distance between the village of Arco de Sao Jorge, my exact location on the island, and the village of my own childhood, situated in the sub-Carpathian region of Romania, is more than 3,700 kilometres. To get from one place to the other, one needs to cross most of the European continent and to advance quite a bit into the Atlantic Ocean. These two places are so far apart that they might as well be on different planets. Yet, one reminds me of the other. They both have in common the lush vegetation, the rural tranquillity, and a slower pace of life.

Madeira is beautiful, wild, endlessly charming, and scary, when I think of it. Being stranded on top of a volcanic rock in the middle of the ocean, far away from mainland, makes me more aware of how minuscule and transient human life is in relation to the rest of the universe. A vessel floating on endless waters, one angry wave away from disaster. But for now, the air is warm and pleasant. A peaceful summer's day.

Happy journey

The only time I remember having heard someone say *I am happy* was from a nun in her eighties, an inhabitant of a distant Portuguese island.

Her circumstances were not perfect, as she had recently lost one more of her siblings and her only blood sister still alive was having serious health issues.

It seems, however, that I had to go far away from the mainland, in the middle of the ocean, in order to hear someone say aloud that she is happy, and this because of living close to God and serving God for over 64 years of her existence.

This humble woman, looking more than

twenty years younger, taught me several very timely lessons:

- that we do not have to wait for the circumstances of our lives to be perfect in order to be happy;

- that people can age gracefully, so there is no need to be so afraid of getting old;

- that cultivating the spiritual dimension of our existence, through whichever channel comes most naturally to our being, will make us happy and potentially assist us in utilizing fully our journey in the flesh.

The secret to such blissful embrace of life, with all of its joys and sorrows, seems to consist in assigning a higher purpose to our earthly existence and living every day according to such belief.

Fall into the inner darkness

An acquaintance was telling me the other day about how his brother-in-law had tried to kill himself with a kitchen knife but failed. *He's been a failure all his life,* he said. That man is depressive and so is his wife.

My acquaintance's family has a history of depression. Other relatives would lie in bed and only get up to wash themselves and go to work. Their depression was *milder*. My acquaintance's sister and her husband took it to a whole new level: attempted suicide.

I had times when I could place myself at the mild end of depression. I would hardly do anything productive beside going to work. For some reason *at work* I was functioning just fine; not so in my personal life.

Depression seems to be a fall in your inner darkness, like being absorbed into a black whole. The only escape is interaction with other human beings. Yet, that is exactly what you run away from when feeling down. At those times, bringing yourself to say *Hello!* and *How are you?* to another person seems an insurmountable task. Work on the other hand forces you to get out there and face the other, whether you feel like it or not. This can be your lifeline, your anchor into reality.

What happens then if you are depressive and hate your job or your boss? One more reason to kill yourself. You can range it up there with having a disagreement with your spouse- type of reasons needed to want to put an end to it all.

When you are depressed, any inconvenience turns into a drama and soon the only exit is the Exit. Unless you are one of those people whose instinct for self-preservation is much stronger than any pain felt so far, or again you are not really depressed, just sad, anxious, and lost. Aren't we all a bit like that?

Animals are nourishment

Humans and animals are meant to live in each other's company. We found each other on this vast planet, none of us knowing for sure why we are here and how we have appeared. The difference resides in the fact that animals don't seem to be aware or to care, for that matter, about all the issues with which humans choose to fill their minds. Due to their ignorance, animals appear to us as innocent and maybe this is the reason why some of us enjoy spending time in their company, even more so than in the company of fellow human beings.

Animals are contributing to both our spiritual and our physical nourishment. My companion animal nourishes my soul, while the chicken breast I had for dinner has hopefully nourished my body. Which animal is intended for which purpose, this is down to the individual animal's destiny and to human custom.

And then, there are the unrealistic animal lovers, the type of persons who say that we should stop eating cows, sheep, and pigs because they are cuddly and sentient. Yes they are, but if we didn't intend to eat them, nobody would want to raise and feed them just so that they can be kept as pets. Most domestic species that we are so familiarized with today would go extinct if we gave up eating meat. Not to mention that sustainable agriculture necessarily incorporates animals. Imagine keeping a cow as a pet. Unpractical, unless you live in India in a society built around worshiping cows as sacred, or you own an animal shelter.

For a long time, I, too, have been struggling with the idea that, in order for me to eat meat, a living, breathing, innocent being has to be put to death. At one point in my life, I gave up eating any kind of meat (also fish, of course) for a whole year, motivated by my deep dislike for human-caused animal deaths. Undoubtedly, that year, I was the most annoying vegetarian in town. Certainly, in keeping with my nature, I couldn't possibly be content with just making my own food choices and letting the others eat what they please, according to their consciousness. I was proselytising right and left, especially at lunch time, when I was eating with my work colleagues.

Unfortunately, that year, I also discovered that maintaining a balanced diet while excluding almost all foods of animal origin is not so straightforward as one may think. It requires a bit of planning and a lot of action, and I am the type of person that doesn't like to spend too much time engaging in food consumption-related activities, for the simple reason that I am always good at discovering a myriad other things that I would much rather do. My vegetarian diet had become unmanageable because I was giving up more and more foods of animal origin (the eggs for instance were making me sick), and I wasn't replacing them with much else besides potatoes.

These days, I am no longer a vegetarian, but I remain deeply aware that I need to limit my meat intake as much as possible, in the interest of health and for the sake of the animals that are raised and killed, most of the time, in some god-awful conditions. Ideally, I should raise and butcher my own meat; such is my understanding of a conscientious carnivore. My grandparents were doing just that. They were raising and butchering their own animals, which didn't make them heartless people. In fact, they cared deeply for their animals because their life and livelihood depended on them.

We are certainly no more compassionate than them just because most of us couldn't summon enough gumption to cut off a rooster's head, even if our life depended on it. We are just choosing to ignore the source of that which fuels our bodies on a daily basis, but we do so at our own peril. Such a complete surrender of control in respect to one of life's essential needs, food, would seem to our ancestors rather inexplicable and foolish.

Childhood and other musings

I will tell you a story. It was happening in the eighties. This was the decade of the twentieth century when John Lennon was assassinated, Saddam Hussein launched a decade-long war on Iran over resources, AIDS and Prozac were discovered, François Mitterrand, Helmut Kohl, and Margaret Thatcher were shaping the European political landscape, the hole in the ozone layer became a certainty, the Challenger exploded, and the Ninja Turtles enchanted kids the world round.

During most of those years, my childhood was happening in a green village tucked away somewhere in the sub-Carpathian region of

Romania. I had been thrown into the world in a country ruled by a dictator, but I knew and cared little about him. Childhood and rural existence occupy their own time and space, which overlap only partially with the present. They shelter you from ugliness. They did shelter me some.

I was raised in part by my grandparents. When I didn't spend time in their farmhouse, I was back in the two-bedroom apartment from a communist-style block of flats, in a small provincial town, with my mother and father, my sister and brother. But I was always longing for the green hills and for my grandparents' farmhouse.

That house is now deserted. My grandfather passed away about ten years before my grandmother. He died just as discreetly as he had lived. He was disappearing like a candle with every passing day, consumed by cancer. During his last days, he was frequently sitting outside, on the concrete stairs leading to the main kitchen, silently contemplating the nature that was burgeoning all around him without any concern for his private tragedy. Maybe he was doing this in anticipation of the huge plunge into nature that was awaiting him.

As for my grandmother, I was nowhere near her at the end of her journey, nor did I attend her funeral. Out of cowardice of course. I let the space protect me from her agony and death. *I don't like funerals*, I would reply on a defensive tone to whomever would inquire about my absence. But does anyone? *Funerals give me nightmares.* Hers gave me nightmares anyway, but I got over them and moved on. Memory is an unfaithful woman. My memory is particularly flighty and disloyal. Yet through these lines I will coerce her to help me resurrect some of the moments of my lovely childhood.

While looking at the sky with perpetually shifting colours and in general at the wonderfully diverse natural world, I found myself regretting not once that God did not bequeath on me a talent for painting. I could have captured that light, that gracious beauty of a fleeting instant and render it on a canvas for myself and for others to enjoy over and over again. More so with people's faces and their whole being that so despairingly elude us once they are too far away, somewhere on the face of the earth, or two meters under it.

My grandmother, was a fleshy woman hobbling around the house all day long. Her right foot was a bit stiff after a surgery undergone in her youth. Round face, green eyes, she liked to talk a lot and would get rather bossy with her family. She definitely overshadowed her husband, my late grandfather, a short but still handsome man with a pronounced taste for alcohol. Every autumn, my grandfather was preparing the precious plum brandy by himself. Now that I think of him I can feel for a moment the ghost of that smell of brandy. My grandfather was a reserved man with a quick mind. He had been some kind of shop administrator in his youth and after that a mere construction worker. This is where he might have picked up his taste for drinking. Above all a peasant, he had built his house with his own hands and, with his wife's help, he had raised two children, kept some domestic animals, and worked the land.

(Haymaking day with my grandparents, my brother, and my sister - 1990s, Wallachia region, Romania)

I cannot say that I knew my grandfather very well. He worked in the fields and his wife around the house. In this manner, I ended up spending most of my time with my grandmother. She annoyed him a lot, especially since he had taken up drinking heavily. Maybe even before, but I wasn't around then to testify.

Drinking made him more talkative and, in my grandmother's opinion, more inefficient in his work, and thus poorer. But he was not an aggressive man, which is of some importance to me. Not to my grandmother. She would fight, complain, and cry, anything to force him to quit drinking, but to no avail.

How I hated those fights. It seemed that I never managed to get away from them wherever I went. Without them, my childhood would have been closer to perfection, out there in the scented hills. Yet, is there anything perfect in this world?

In any case, I enjoyed my time in my

grandparents' village. I knew most of the old ladies and their husbands who had houses on the same street. We were related to some of them. I had much affection in particular for one of my grandfather's sisters and her husband. They always helped us when we needed their support. They were there for us right from the beginning and until the bitter end. Bitter indeed it was. When my grandmother started getting strokes, they would visit her daily to check on her condition and they even brought her food. I had this idea in my head that this female relative of ours had a similar facial expression to a popular (male!) singer of the time. She was blond, blue eyes, and such a gentle and joyful little woman. She has since died peacefully in her sleep. The fitting death, if ever there was one, of a very gentle soul. I remember her blond smile.

When the characters that populated my childhood started to disappear, I finally realized that I was getting old.

Gradually, all the people whose presence was a daily reality in my childhood years have dropped from the firmament like stars. They used to be enormous in my life, then with the passing of the years and my distancing from home, they started to decrease in size until becoming mere blips on the radar. One by one, silently and humbly, they faded away.

It is curious how their passing would only trigger some anodyne remarks in discussions with family members, as well as a slight increase in my fear of darkness for a while. I am aware that they deserve so much more. But caught in the torrent of life, I slide forward and leave them behind, barely acknowledging their existence and nowadays non-existence.

We grow indifferent to the life and death of people that used to be so dear to us. Space and time expand between us to the point that we become strangers to one another. Maybe this is nature's way of preparing us to accept the other's mortality. It lightens the burden, sometimes.

Promise you will never leave me behind

You are among those very rare people
who can tolerate the real me long enough.
I don't know why this is.
I feel that you have brought a spark in my life
that was not there before.
I suppose I like myself better,
the *me* I've become since I've met you.
There is a childlike spring in my step
I'm afraid I would lose if I were to lose you.
Promise you will never leave me behind.

Maybe this is who I really am.
A lost child too afraid to be abandoned,
an awkward child who only hopes to be accepted

by someone long enough.

Too many times abandoned,

too intensely lonely most of the time.

With your presence in my life,

I feel that I can go through most things

and achieve a lot.

Promise you will never leave me behind.

Anatomy of a job announcement

The job announcement reads as follows:

You are a positive thinker, progress oriented, a flexible team worker and able to manage stressful situations.

With this one sentence, not particularly original if I may add, the potential employer indicates that they intend to crash your free spirit, should you have any left.

Positive thinker means that you will keep a straight face while they pile an awful lot of indifferent (to you) work on your back and turn every single day of your life into a miserable simulacrum of existence. The equivalent of the old adage *serving with a smile*. By *progress oriented*, they refer to the progress of their endeavour and the enrichment of their shareholders, at the expense of your sanity. *A flexible team member* means that you must put up with annoying colleagues. *Able to manage stressful situations* means just that, your work days will cause you a lot of anguish, which will then bleed into your free time and your family life. And this will lead you on the shrink's couch and in the courtroom, in any order you may prefer.

And for an entry-level secretarial job, they require the following:

You have an excellent command of French and English, a good knowledge in German, additional language skills such as (insert language spoken by a handful of people on the entire face of the earth) *are an asset.*

In the past, famous philosophers and statesmen where polyglots, nowadays any secretary must become one too, if she hopes to feed her family in a modern *multicultural* city.

And so the description of the ideal secretary

continues with:

You are well organized, flexible, and have excellent communication skills.

You should be young, beautiful, and know how to whisper the right words into the right ears. The word *flexible* returns obsessively, since one can never stress enough the importance of an easily bent mind, or body, or both, as the situation may call for.

I feel that nowadays most people's approach to the employee lifestyle is alas perfectly summed up by the saying: *damned if you do and damned if you don't.* After all, what options do we have? Sure you are free to change one set of handcuffs for another by changing employers, but that doesn't get you out of the race. You also have the option to go the independent route, which is surely covered by the bones of many valiant knights, as you will soon discover. And if you still prefer to eat, after all is said and done, you will humbly return to your employer.

So far, my response to this catch-22 sort of situation has been to hope for the best and prepare for the worst. In practice, it means that when I have adequate wages, I always try to save aggressively, and mind you aggressively does not mean 10%/15%, but as much as I can bear, without starving and depriving myself of any pleasure in life. At times, I was able to save 80%/90% of my salary, or even more. This can be achieved with an adequate amount of salary and with parallel streams of income, as apparently insignificant as they may be, because they do add up. Saving at the tune of 80%/90% may not sound like much fun for everyone, but I can assure you that when the lean times come, and they always come, and I have some savings and no debt to my name, then I can ride the period on my additional streams of income and get out by the other side of the tunnel without too much fuss.

In addition to saving, there are other measures one can take: continue to educate yourself so you can remain employable, freelance, or start a business; keep in touch with your former colleagues; don't trade on the stock exchange (or play Russian roulette, as I call it) in any serious manner, unless you are a professional; avoid any major addictions (drinking, drugs, gambling, prostitutes); don't bring into the world more children than you can realistically afford to raise; stay out of debt or pay up your debts as fast as possible, and so forth. Of course, you may come up with your own solutions. These are just a few common-sense measures, but I find it unbelievable how many people never come around to applying them in any serious, consistent manner.

Who can break this cycle?

There is a secret war going on mostly away from the cameras, behind closed doors. Many people aren't even aware of it and those who are, conveniently choose to forget it. It is called domestic violence, continuous aggression inflicted by a member of the household on the spouse and/or the rest of the family.

Battered women can try to find refuge in shelters, but few are those who will take advantage of the helping hand extended by society. For most of them this is not really an option. First of all, an aggressive partner will not give up only because he has been temporarily removed from the close proximity of his family. He will most likely threaten and terrify his victim to such an extent that she will never even seriously consider an escape. This subtle or not so subtle regime of terror is built in time and engenders a unique relationship between victim and aggressor, almost complicity and dependence, a vicious circle. In addition, there are economic concerns that frequently force the woman to put up with this lifestyle, especially when children are involved. In the economically disadvantaged portions of the society, but not only there, a lot of courage, initiative, and a particularly supportive entourage would be required for a battered woman to escape her aggressor, especially if she is a mother.

The situation of the children involved in such a seemingly never-ending drama is even more distressing. They feel helpless in a chaotic world, trapped between two adults perpetually entangled in a destructive fight.

Scientists and social workers only begin to

grasp the complex impact such a poisoned environment has on children growing up with domestic violence. A word describes them well, *traumatised*. But here ends the straightforward description of these children. Mainly because they can react differently to their environment depending on factors such as age, length of exposure, personality, interaction with siblings, and support elements from the society.

Sadly the effects of domestic violence on children are lasting and get carried over into adulthood engendering in their turn all kinds of difficulties more or less subtle and even perpetuating the cycle of violence. Individuals who grew up in troubled families are more likely to experience difficulties while trying to integrate into society as fully functioning and productive human beings. This is not to say that they will turn by necessity into abusive parents and spouses, criminals, or live on the welfare. Most frequently they do not. On the contrary, they are inclined to try hard to forge a future for themselves and build a stable and healthy family, the kind they were denied. Nevertheless their scars are never quite healed and those of us who are more watchful will secretly have the intuition of their private struggle where other people fail to see a thing.

With all of its negative consequences, having had a troubled childhood can also carry with it, to some extent, positive aspects. A person who was subject to unhappy circumstances early on will either raise above them, toughen up in some ways, or will surrender to the evil in the world. One can go through life strong and a little scared at the same time. In any event the sensitivity thus gained may transform the soul of an otherwise ordinary person and fill it with compassion.

Finally, let's look at the aggressor. Most often than not he is plagued by some mental disorder or addiction. His altered state of mind, combined with the harsh economic realities of life, operates against the backdrop of a society which tolerates, if not openly encourages, disciplining of women by their spouses. All of these circumstances allow an apparently ordinary man to inflict indescribable suffering, both physical and emotional, on the people who are closest to him, his family. His wife and children are naturally easy preys, guaranteed to remain so over the years. In most cases, the aggressor will live his entire life undisclosed and unchallenged. To further complicate matters, he is not necessarily a heartless person. This is often the case of a more or less troubled individual whom the society, through its specialized institutions, has failed to educate and assist early on. Left to his own devices, or even encouraged by a climate of lenience towards the perpetrators of violence against women, he has turned against his own.

Every family represents a very delicate ecosystem. Abrupt intrusion from the outside cannot magically resolve all of its troubles. However, society has a duty to eradicate the scourge of domestic violence. In this day and age, it is our collective responsibility to make it more difficult, if not entirely impossible, for any person to inflict with impunity unspeakable suffering on his own family.

Equality

In the course of history, all manner of abuse has been perpetrated under the banner of marriage and family, as it is the case with other holy institutions. The solution does not reside, of course, in discarding the institution of marriage altogether, as some forces in our world work hard to achieve, but in exposing its greatest sins so that they may be eliminated.

In general, abuse occurs when some human beings are encouraged or permitted to believe that they are superior to or more entitled than others. Family in its patriarchal forms suffers from the supposed superiority of husband over wife (and possibly over children), or that of male sibling over female sibling. Such differentiation is believed to originate at birth: one is superior by the simple fact of being born a male. This hierarchical classification of human beings on the sole basis of gender means in practice more obligations for women and more rights for men.

As the society modernises and slowly moves away from such outdated ideas, the inequalities persist in the professional and social arena. Some men and women are more entitled than others due to gender, nationality, race, social status, and mostly because of being born under different, more auspicious circumstances, because of associating with people in that position, or having access to more resources. Birth and resources continue to divide us, while death is the big equalizer. Communism also preaches equality, but the problem there, as with all man-made systems, is that some are more equal than others. In front of death, we no longer have this issue.

Painting, living and other lost arts

Painting forces our mind to concentrate on the present moment. In that respect, I suppose it has something to do with the now wildly fashionable concept of mindfulness.

Moreover, painting is a peaceful endeavour that gets us in touch with our inner child, which is not to say that it represents a childish activity. For me, watercolour painting is akin to writing poetry. Both deal with delicate matter.

The art of painting can also be compared to any other activity that captures one's attention and sparks one's creativity, be it spinning wool by hand, knitting, gardening, cooking a great meal for one's family, taking care of animals or children, or so many other human activities, which, even though not readily classified as art, become artistic merely by the engrossment and the creativity with which a human being is practicing them.

Busy hands stop the mind from wandering away into dark and scary places. Maybe this is why traditional rural communities experienced low rates of depression and suicide.

The hands-on involvement with the world around them, the higher level of control exercised over their time and livelihood, and the belonging to a tight-knit community may have contributed to the superior life satisfaction enjoyed by our ancestors. Surprisingly, the modern world, in exchange for (cheap) comfort and entertainment, deprives us of the very elements that make human life enjoyable and worth living. Trips abroad, shopping, partying, going to the movies, meals at restaurants, driving fast cars, social media, large sugar intake, these are all activities that are supposed to make the modern human happy. Except that none of these things provides lasting satisfaction. They trigger short spikes of pleasure that die out as soon as the experience has ended and the person has returned to the daily grind. As a consequence, people seek a constant renewal of their external-induced pleasures: more trips, more shopping, more social media, more junk. In order to satisfy such artificial needs, they must work longer and more intensely at jobs that they despise. They effectively waste their most valuable resource, their time on earth.

Our society functions on the same principle as crack cocaine, it is highly addictive and all-consuming. Not much of a path to happiness.

Our turn, tomorrow?

Lying for days, for months, for a whole year alone on a hospital bed. People come and go. She remains still, left behind. What are the thoughts passing through her mind? There must have been thoughts in the beginning at least, because later on, I think she just gives up reflecting on things and lives in the moment, and sleeps a lot.

The days resemble each other, punctuated by the arrival of the nurses who attend to her physiological needs. After that, she just stares at the empty walls and eventually sleeps. Are there dreams in her sleep? What would you dream of if you were old, sick, and abandoned on a dirty hospital bed? Maybe she dreams of her childhood and of her youth. Old people tend to take refuge in their early memories. Those are the memories that survive after strokes. Those are the few belongings that we carry into the sunset of our lives.

Does she ever accuse us, her family, for letting her lie there all alone? I did not catch any accusatory glance the rare times I ever visited her. In the beginning, when her mind was still lucid, her face would only display silent joy and gratefulness - I imagined - for seeing us come visit her. I know vaguely that she did not want to be taken to the hospital in the first place, but she must have given in and accepted the situation.

On the bed next to her, there is an older woman very thin and weak. That woman's mind is no longer coherent. She already lives in a completely imaginary world, imaginary to us, that is, because in fact she is living her younger days, inhabiting her farmhouse, dealing with domestic animals and daily chores. I offer her a slice or two of the sponge cake that I brought for my relative. She eats it avidly spilling a myriad of crumbles all over her bed. She asks me to help her change the position of a tired body turned stiff by the approach of death. I am happy to help, even if a bit embarrassed by the rancid smell coming from the sheets. I am ashamed of my embarrassment.

I turn my attention to the person I came to visit. I exchange some small talk with her. I feel so useless and unpractical. Selfish too. Eventually I leave her there and go save myself in the buzzing world outside, promising that I will be back soon. The last time I passed by her hospital bed in this pilgrimage of pity and guilt, I must have uttered the same vague promise: *I will come back to see you soon*. Though not soon enough for her burial ceremony.

She had been semi-abandoned in the psychiatric ward of a small town hospital. Then, once death was looming, she was taken back to her home, so she could pass away.

Imprisoned souls

The characters that populate the prisons of our nations are human beings, too. Sometimes the sins of those locked up are less heavy that the ones being carried by individuals from outside the walls. Who is to know the real soul of every man?

By now, we are well aware that law and ethics fail to overlap most of the time. If we became a bit more humble and sensitive to the error of our own ways, we would not be so quick to cast the proverbial stone.

Among other causes, radical economic discrepancies within the society, as well as living without being able to put down roots, increase the incidence of unlawful activities. In our globalized world, where the media constantly bombards us with fabricated images and news, we do not compare ourselves only to our immediate neighbours, but also to the economic situation of social groups from other countries, even from other continents. This causes dissatisfaction, especially among young people living in disadvantaged communities and poor nations. The ensuing migration for economic reasons triggers, both in the countries of origin and in the target countries, more inequality and criminal activity.

Poverty and dislocation breed crime. A person experiencing poverty and dislocation is pushed towards the edges of the normalised social existence. And since the legal system is meant to defend the established social order, such a person quickly comes into conflict with the law. In our heavily regulated society, those who cannot or do not wish to conform find themselves criminalised.

Therefore, the imprisonment of the offenders,

even though it seems to be the preferred solution, does not get to root of the problem. If anything, the issues are likely to deepen in direct relation to the increase in the number of penitentiaries.

If you have a pain in your arm, will you cut your arm down, or rather try to find the cause of the pain and treat it so that the arm heals?

An exercise in positive thinking

At any given moment, beauty and ugliness intertwine in our world like the fetid corpse of a rat decomposing right next to a patch of daffodils in full bloom.

Pettiness, arrogance and cruelty of ignorant people invested with some authority over their fellow human beings, mental disease, lack of resources for lack of wanting to play the game of the *modern* society, poverty and immense richness passing each other in the streets with total indifference- all of these in a day make one rather pessimistic about the human condition.

Fortunately, there are also other days and experiences meant to partially reconcile us with our fate.

Either way, walking the earth as a living being is no walk in the park. Don't let the modern preachers of *positive thinking* tell you otherwise. They are in the business of deceit and infantilisation.

Because of the shallow approach to life so persistent in our culture, focused on eternal youth, material success, and sexual promiscuity, we are unprepared to face the very real challenges that we are all bound to encounter sooner or later.

We don't know how to live for lack of knowledge of how we should die. Old age and death are hushed in polite conversations, while over-amplified in the media. At the end, we are left to deal with them as they come over us, at the tune of heavy doses of anxiolytics or by hiding our collective head in the sand.

Whether inside modern offices, behind the wheel of expensive cars, or holding every selfie-stick that roams the streets of our cities, there must be legions of humans that have never grown up. They are intent on carrying their childish whims all the way to the grave.

I do not feel mature myself, even though I may have already used almost half of my available time on this earth (according to my own optimistic estimation!). If my approach to greying hair is any indication, I am blatantly unprepared to face old age and the accompanying decline. For the time being, my solution to greying hair is to promptly pluck out the offenders. I will have to resort to other means of retaliation once the relentless enemy finally gets the better of me. And then, if I am lucky, there will come a time when greying hair will be the least of my concerns.

View from the meadow

I'm lying on the grass looking at the clear summer's sky, with a book on my side. No other human in sight, just the endless pastures, the trees, the hills, and the blue sky.

A few meters away there is my cow, well in fact my grandparents' cow. She is grazing peacefully. The only dominant sound is the cow's rhythmically munching of the grass and, from time to time, the savage whip of her tail with which she is trying to defend herself from insects.

The year must be 1994, or any other year for that matter from the second half of the 1980s through the first half of the 1990s. I am spending my summer holidays in my grandparents' village and one of my tasks, you guessed it, consists of taking their cow to graze on the pastures surrounding the village.

For people living in the countryside there is always something to do around the house or in the fields, and everybody needs to contribute to the running of the homestead, even the children. Presented with the opportunity, I had naturally fallen into the activity of grazing sheep and cattle, because it allowed me to do what I enjoy the most, reading and daydreaming. This task also incorporated my other passions, nature and animals.

In fact, I happen to be one of those strange people who believe that cows have beautiful eyes. Have you ever looked into the eyes of a cow? Technically one can only look into one eye at a time, since they have them on separate sides of the skull like all pray animals. You should give it a try. Cows look at us through these huge puddles in brown and black hues. Their eyes exude calm, tenderness, and melancholy. At least, such were the eyes of the brown cow from my childhood.

Later on, while in school, a male teacher was sharing with us his difficulties to find a suitable spouse, and he mentioned among other things, to the endless amusement of the entire class, that you cannot compliment a woman saying that her eyes are as beautiful as the eyes of a cow. She wouldn't take it well (the woman, not the cow). I remember thinking that surely the woman in question wasn't familiarised enough with these gentle creatures in order to fully appreciate the compliment. It wasn't the cow's loss. Truthfully, it seemed that our teacher needed to brush up on his pick-up lines as well.

New spring

"Spring is my favourite season", she said.
He already knew that about her because at the beginning of every spring she never failed to point it out, in more or less the same words, her face beaming with a large innocent smile.

Birds, populating in growing numbers the woods,
joyfully welcome the slow arrival of spring.
With every passing day,
leaves of perennial flowers
spring up more intensely green.
I take in the stillness of the air
and the trees,
the low light of the approaching evening,

the view of a small group of nuns,

walking on the peaceful path of their garden.

Like a flock of blue birds,

they show up shyly from another age,

then vanish again at the sound of church bells.

A surreal performance

solely intended for my eyes.

Not far away, traffic continues unabated,

marking the detached rhythm of modern times.

Bread and circuses

To this day and whether they are aware of it or not, many people still get married and procreate because they are expected to; they go to school and hold onto jobs for decades, for the sole purpose of fulfilling other people's expectations of them.

Today, as in the past, individuals yield to group pressure more often than not, even though the group has abdicated much of its responsibility for the individual's wellbeing. In a modern cosmopolitan city I stumble upon similar prejudices to those I would find in a remote village. However, unlike in the case of the village where your neighbours would not only force you to abide by the rules of the community, but also assist you in your need, in large urban areas the individual must fend for himself. Most often than not, everybody is on his own and nobody, except perhaps a small circle of family and friends, if they happen to live in your proximity, care about you and are ready to lend you a helping hand.

Behind the veneer of luxury, entertainment, and modern efficiency, the large towns in which many of us live and work nowadays remain harsh places, especially for those enduring poverty and loneliness. People try to build a simulacrum of community. Leisure activities and groups dedicated to them abound. Yet, in the end, everybody comes and goes so fast that they fail to establish lasting connections. They are all incredibly busy running around in circles, trying to keep a roof over their head. On every given day, two subjects seem to dominate the thoughts of the urban dwellers: money and holidays.

It is considered desirable to spend the few weeks of paid freedom from toil, generously granted by our employers, engaged in frenetic touristic activities in a distant (and the more exotic the better) place. But what is the reason for this mad dash for the nearest airport or highway, as soon as the clock marks the end of the workday and the beginning of the holidays? I am not able to understand it otherwise than as a phenomenon of fashion and an indication of dissatisfaction with everyday existence.

Meanwhile, those who, for financial reasons, are unable to partake in this almost religious celebration of freedom feel left out and even more dissatisfied with their lives.

However, there are other ways to celebrate life besides packing every waking hour with money-generating activities during our working days and money-wasting activities during our periods of leisure, as a sort of mindless embodiment of the *work hard play hard* mantra promoted by those who can profit every time from such an arrangement.

Essentially, it all comes down to this: if we accepted to indulge in less money-spending activities during our free time or at all times, we would have to work less arduously to gain money in the first place. It is not a matter of depriving oneself, or of being less ambitious in our professional lives. We can of course continue to work as hard as we want, but by cutting-down on superficial pleasures, we can afford the luxury to work as much as we want at things that bring us real satisfaction or, alternatively, we can reduce the time we must engage in less than ideal work arrangements. As a consequence, our everyday life should improve and we wouldn't need to wait for the weekends, for the holidays, or for our employer's permission in order to live our life. On a Monday morning a human being should be as happy to be alive as on a Saturday morning.

The following scene unfolds at lunchtime in a bustling business neighbourhood: numerous suit-clad people are taking to the streets for a hurried lunch away from their prestigious office jobs and, in their midst, several stall vendors are displaying their merchandise and making some sales. When comparing these two types of workers, which of them seem to have more control over their time and thus more freedom? Maybe some people from both categories, maybe none of them, maybe just the owners of their respective places of business enjoy real control and freedom.

There are many ways to make a living. Thus we should strive to find the way that suits us best. It is tempting to think that we do not have a choice, when in reality we often do, but it takes guts, perseverance, even a bit of madness in order to break free from the mould of society and live purposefully once again.

Be the best that you can be

I believe that at this stage in human history, particularly in the *civilised* world, we should be able to choose the type of work and life that allows us to use our talents at the highest level, to fulfil our destiny, to achieve our highest potential. Indeed, as human beings, we have a duty to become, in our lifetime, the best version of what we can be, both from a material and a spiritual point of view.

Should we choose to pursue such an objective, we will find it easier to achieve if we are able at times to accept less pay for our work, or to change employment when it is no longer fulfilling, or even to live our lives without being tied down by full-time employment. The higher purpose of discovering and actualizing our true potential as human beings should motivate us to get our financial life in order as much and as soon as possible, instead of being trapped under increasingly heavier financial obligations with very little wiggle room, which in turn would force us to focus on mere survival.

In this context, striving for financial autonomy is a worthwhile endeavour. A certain degree of freedom from financial worries opens up a world of opportunities in a person's life.

You may think by now that this is all well and good, you would certainly enjoy having less financial worries, but unfortunately you were not born in a wealthy family, you did not win the lottery, you are not extremely intelligent, or even beautiful, or particularly hard working for that matter, in order to get a break in life. So you conclude that there is no hope for you other than work in soul-wrenching jobs until retirement or death, and you should resign yourself to this *reality* and consider yourself lucky to have a job or benefit from a retirement plan. This is the lot of the ordinary people.

There are people in the world who started out just like any of us, but along the way they decided, or they felt compelled to achieve more than the ordinary, to take life in their own hands and live it more consciously than their peers.

As human beings, we have great capacities for thinking, creating, dreaming, loving, sacrificing, fighting, all of these being interconnected with a good number of weaknesses. Any regular person with regular abilities has great power within himself or herself, and must fight many pitfalls. We certainly use those powers in key moments of our lives, when struggling with a serious disease, facing the death of a loved one, giving birth, facing catastrophic events, to name just a few. The rest of the time we coast through life seeking pleasure and avoiding pain.

It would be interesting to imagine what would happen if we got in the habit of tapping into our internal resources more willingly and not only when forced by extraordinary outside circumstances. Resignation is not a way to live, even though I have the feeling that we are trained all our life to accept just that. Of course we operate within the time constraints imposed by our human condition, we are born, we live, and then we die. Society also places a myriad other constraints on us. We may accept, up to a certain degree, some of them, reject others, while enjoying the advantages afforded by our belonging to the social fabric.

However, we must distinguish between constraint and opportunity. Not all limitations placed on us by other people, past or present, are to be accepted indiscriminately and obeyed. In addition, there are those limitations we place on ourselves, those existing only in our imagination or as a result of our own actions. The idea that we cannot have access to financial autonomy is one such self-defeating attitude, or that we cannot achieve anything of great value in our lifetime because we are just ordinary people. Indeed, things of value can only be attained through effort, and they take time. They come at a price. But resignation to one's faith also comes at a price. We shall become fully aware of what the price may be in the long term for the choices we make today, then make those choices with all our might.

In order to gain the freedom needed to search for a higher life purpose, we must learn, among other things, how to effectively manage our resources. We can give ourselves the most precious gift of all, the gift of time, by adopting a more simple and efficient lifestyle. Let us start by practicing the unfashionable art of saying NO to our inflated *needs*, our inflated ego, as well as to other people's unreasonable requests on our time and energy, all the while remembering that, most of the time, we alone are in the driver's seat of our life.

Whatever happened to critical thinking

Consumerism has become so ingrained in our existence, that even in the realm of ideas people tend to shop around for a pre-packaged opinion on everything, from the way our countries should be governed to who should be voted the best singer in the latest Eurovision song contest.

Information seems abundant and free, and we are incessantly bombarded by it due to the ubiquitous use of communication technology. Furthermore, the modern human being is incredibly busy, sometimes for good reason because we all need to make a living; many times though we are just expending energy on useless or insignificant stuff. In these conditions, no wonder most of us don't have time or inclination to stop and reflect deeply on our own lives or on what is going on in this big interconnected world of ours. Hence the propensity to embrace pre-packaged ideas, opinions, causes. Besides, the need to belong is very deeply ingrained in us, and so radical ideas would effectively place us at odds with our group of choice.

We have been told that we must keep abreast of what is going on in the world at all times. So we religiously follow the news, whether on TV, in the newspapers, or through the social media feeds. The problem is that this ready-made information is delivered to us by the corporations who run the media or by various influence groups. So, we cannot possibly believe that all of it is objective or complete. Then, what is the purpose of consuming it every single day?

In order to enhance our critical thinking, among other benefits, we would be well served to take a distance from *the events* once in a while. Call it a news sabbatical of sorts. The advantages are manifold.

First, most things that are considered newsworthy are bound to be negative: wars, terrorist attacks, diseases, political battles, natural disasters, and so forth. Feeding our brain with a steady diet of apocalyptic images, words, and sounds cannot possibly be healthy for us. So no wonder we suffer from anxiety, depression, and other mental issues in such great numbers. Plus, just looking at the atrocities on our screens is rather useless if we do not take any action to change something for the better.

Secondly, if we protect our psyche from the daily onslaught of information, we are more likely to have a fresh understanding and approach once we decide to analyse events of particular interest to us. By limiting the number of instances we look into, we are more able to exercise our critical thinking by asking many questions and then trying to find answers from various sources. This is the opposite of just reading or watching the news on automatic pilot and then embracing whatever other people have to say.

Many people think that they are indeed analysing critically whatever is served to them by the media and that they have come to their point of view all by themselves. But it just so happens that their *original* opinion is a carbon copy of the opinion of thousands of others who use the same sources of information as themselves.

Social media is successfully and dangerously contributing to the dissemination of pre-packaged ideas and opinions. And because everybody can make his or her views known on these platforms, they are under the impression that whatever is disseminated through such channels is authentic and, if I may call it so, *democratic*. Yet, peer pressure is alive and well also on social media. This becomes more apparent in times of political and social turmoil. In those times when entire nations are swept away by some fabricated slogans aggressively promoted through all available channels by *influencers* of all stripes, one is hard pressed to find valiant souls who dare to communicate, in a democratic fashion, their personal views, if it so happens that those views do not align with the general opinion.

Nowadays, critical thinking remains as dangerous for the status-quo as it has always been. No wonder it is not taught in schools and it is certainly not encouraged in society.

ACKNOWLEDGEMENTS

A heartfelt thank you to my mother, Elena, to my other family members, as well as to my partner, for believing in me and in my dream. My gratitude also goes to those who generously agreed to read, critique, and improve earlier versions of this text.

ABOUT THE AUTHOR

Anca Tudorascu, born in 1980 in Ceausescu's Romania, currently established in the Grand Duchy of Luxembourg with her long term partner, is an author, in addition to her activities of translator, law student, and some other fun stuff. She holds a bachelor's degree in languages and a master's degree in business administration from a Romanian, respectively a French university. She most enjoys, of course, dealing with words, but also spending time with her loved ones, nature, animals, and all things traditional.

You may get in touch with the author at:
www.scribit-traduction.lu

Send her your thoughts about this book
by leaving a review (on Amazon)!

www.ingramcontent.com/pod-product-compliance
Lightning Source LLC
Chambersburg PA
CBHW062118080426
42734CB00012B/2910